A Bad Case of
the Good News

William R. Callahan

To order additional copies of this book — Visit www.quixote.org or call toll-free: 800-746-1160. Bulk discounts are available.

A Bad Case of the Good News by William R. Callahan
ISBN: 978-0-9885194-0-4

Published by Quixote Center, College Park, MD

Book designed & produced by Debra Lipp
Back cover photo by Dolly Pomerleau

DEDICATION

✦

To all who dare to dream dreams
of justice, peace, and equality.

ACKNOWLEDGMENTS

May I thank my gentle friend Sister Rosemarie Canty, CSC, who had the foresight to start collecting Bill's poems 10 years ago? Kathryn McKay graciously read the manuscript and greatly advanced its quality. Thank you, Kathy. And my appreciation goes to Tom Ricker for shepherding this project through to completion. Finally, Debra Lipp, my never less than honest friend and critic (who also makes me laugh), used her designing genius to turn my hodgepodge of text and photos into a beautiful book.

And special thanks to all of you who inspired Bill to write poetry. You have read his poems, been touched by them, and responded with your actions for justice, peace, and equality. You have shared the community that empowered Bill to give his all. He always said that he didn't "want to die all saved up." Well, he didn't.

The gift of his life helped build a world more justly loving.

Gratefully,
Dolly Pomerleau

CONTENTS

✦

✦

INTRODUCTION

This collection of poems by Bill is my tribute to a loved and loving man who opened his heart to all who came within arm's reach. When people were too far away, he shortened the distance by going to them, regardless of risk or insecurity.

These are poems to family, friends, and me. There are poems from Sancho (the Quixote Center's curmudgeon, conservative computer persona), poems about Nicaragua, and the 9/11 attacks. Often, they were written on short notice when I would tell him, "Bill, we need a poem about..." He complied.

There are no poems about his expulsion from the Jesuits or about his Parkinson's Disease. He wrote one for my retirement party in June 2010. The writing is inelligible. He died a month later.

How privileged I am to have shared 40 years of life with this man of justice, full of imagination, brilliant, yet humble — his great qualities too numerous to enumerate — his failures not significant enough to mention.

But you, who also have shared life with Bill, need no explanation.

Bill gave my heart a home wherein it still dwells.

~ *Dolly Pomerleau*

QUIXOTE CENTER

QUIXOTE CENTER

A gathering of people
who work and pray
with laughter
to reach for stars
that seem too distant
to be touched,
or too dim
to be worth
the effort.

We try to be friends
with people in need,
and to celebrate life
with people
who believe that the struggle
to be like Jesus
in building a world
more justly loving
is worth the gift
of our lives.

~ 1976

This poem is the mission statement of the Quixote Center.

PRAISE BE JESUS – WHO LIVES!

Peace and love grow strong
>   when we give our lives to bring them forth.
Jesus, becoming one of us – dares us – cares us
>   into risking the adventure of the Good News
>   which He revealed – and IS!

Justice is to be built, people must be welcomed, clothed,
>   fed and sheltered.
>   It is a joy to share this greatest of quests – with you.

May his peace and love overflow your heart
>   to flood the lives you touch and share.

> ~ *Christmas 1977*

Letter to Quixote Center friends.

TO DONORS: THY PLEDGE

Thy pledge was swift and welcome,
fulfillment has been slow.

We thought we'd write and query
the person who will know.

If our records do prove false
we humbly beg thy pardon.

To serve thee well and warmly
is our goal and guerdon.*

~ 1978

* *guerdon – reward, recompense*

DEAR FRIENDS OF THE QUIXOTE CENTER

Roses are red, violets are blue,
   the Center is broke, how about you?
If you can share the little you own,
   we'll bless and salute you, and work to the bone.

We'll struggle for peace, for justice and jobs,
   and serve in your name, to heal all the sobs.
You'll know in your heart that the money's well spent
   while we pay off the debts and catch up the rent.

We'll organize Christians, and trumpet the call,
   for bold Gospel living of church people, all.
For swords into plowshares, for nuclear freeze,
   'til justice and sharing bring war to its knees.

For sisters and brothers, in equality blest,
   to live and get ready for heavenly rest.
To contemplate noisily earth, God and folks,
   while trusting the Spirit will play us no jokes.

So throughout the day, as you open your hearth, *(pronounce in Bostonese)*
   to the people of God, whom you meet on the path.
Know that we here, on Mt. Rainier's slopes,
   are sharing your dreams, your sorrows and hopes.

Walking together, community strong,
   sharing Christ's joy, as we pilgrim along.
And when we shall gather, midst heavenly dew,
   you vouch for us and we'll vouch for you.

Let's throw a big party, 'round the heavenly throne,
   and celebrate merrily — WE FINALLY GOT HOME!

*Sincerely, Sancho Panza, Esq.**

~ November 1982

* The "Poet Laureate" of the Quixote Center.

DEAR FRIENDS OF SANCHO,

Greetings, my friends in Quixote land
from eagle-eye Sancho, your computer hand!
In case you don't know, I have status and rights;
I'm the senior computer that says it with "bytes!"
I check on the work of this motley crew
so I can report and reassure you.

Politically speaking, I'm off to the right,
but they can't stop my letters which bring you delight.
I'm fond of them too in spite of their bents.
Psychologically speaking, we're co-dependents!

I write to you now with software and mouse,
'cause this crazy bunch just bought them a house.
It's sprawling and ugly — decidedly quaint
by anyone's standards, a beauty it ain't!

I lobbied a mansion or office deluxe,
but these *Quixotistas* responded with yuks!
"Simple and homey," a neighborhood spot,
that's what they looked for; that's what they got!

Four years abandoned; rocks through the glass,
a beached yellow tugboat with no hint of class!
Leaks in the roof matched the holes in their brains,
repairs procreated again and again.

They've patched and they've puttered with caulk and some paint,
and help from some friends who are certainly saints!
They're all deeply grateful to those who send "dough,"
it's helped a great deal, but there's still some to go.

Cause contractors came and contractors went,
leaving big charges ensconced in cement.
They still need some funds 'cause they must pay the bills.
So help, will you please, add a gift to the till!
Fifty, a hundred will further the work.
I'll audit the funds — no money for perks!
Whatever you send, great thanks many fold;
'cause you've brought old Sancho in from the cold!

*Sincerely, Sancho Panza, Esq.**

* The "Poet Laureate" of the Quixote Center.

To
our
friends
across the
continent who
help keep Quixote
programs going with
your volunteer efforts:
To you who collate mailings,
stuff envelopes, and stick labels;
To you who invest time and sweat
packing a box or packing a container;
To you who write letters, make phone calls,
organize events, or undertake studies; To you
who pass the word along; To our friends who
span the globe and make possible the work of the
Center with your physical and financial aid;
May you be
blessed this
Holiday Season.
Thank You!

~ *Christmas 1991* ~

ODE TO DON QUIXOTE

Crazy brained old dreamer,
get a new pair of glasses.
See the ogre as the windmill is.
Let me stand buffer to your imaginings
lest people drown your words in ridicule
which seek to ward off infection by dreamers.

Lest our imagination be yeasted
and we ourselves recruit companions,
saddle up our Rocinantes
and sally forth to noble deeds.

Has anyone seen my glasses?

~ December 2005

Celebrating the 400th anniversary of Cervantes' classic work.

NICARAGUA
QUEST FOR PEACE

A PREFERENTIAL OPTION FOR PEACE

Peace is not the absence of war,
    warriors resting their arms.

Peace is the presence of a love,
    whose arms embrace justice,
        and wrestle
    gentleness from the loam of struggle.

Peace well-springs when people risk
    a preferential option
        a choice to love,
          to turn a bold cheek
    to the blue-steel barrel, the bomb,
        or the blow.

Peace erupts when communities claim love
    and reconciliation,
        forge firm hearts,
           the dream of peace,
    that neither cross nor threat can sunder.

When this bellicose heresy holds sway,
guns furrow bread lands,
        children lead,
        the lions guard the lambs,
    and love's fire roars fierce.

~ March 1992

RECONCILIATION'S HOPE

How often, forgive I should,
    a sister, a brother — seven times?
Maybe three strikes and you're out
    is better yet —
        baseball's gift to social policy.

And the merry voice came back,
    "seventy times seven."
"But that is too hard."
"With human beings, yes,
    but with God's grace, all is possible."
The mighty know better,
    and know nothing at all.
Crusades, jihads, pogroms, holocausts,
    ethnic cleansing, excommunication,
    silencing, repression, torture,
    witness the rich wreckage of their insights.

Anything except apology.
Everything except forgiveness.
Only the broken hearted seem strong enough
    to risk loving an enemy
    for the sake of both's children,
Only God's poor can "shoot the moon"
    and dare the total prize of reconciling love.

~ March 1994

BOLD DREAMERS

Name us women,
flaring imaginations,
dreams writ large,
spinning our hopes,
web traps, snaring,
crafting freedom.

We are butterfly wings on migration,
beating the tireless air,
infecting allies, healing partners,
wringing cooperative capital
with iron arms grown strong
cradling children,
wresting survival
from the macho jaws of hunger
and discrimination.

Join us as bold dreamers,
loosing your fire upon the earth,
forging visions,
militant lambs hugging lions,
treasuring all with joyful hearts.
Join us.

~ 1995

REGADIO

Simple dream, really.
Light for the night,
turning for the mill,
water from the pump,
electricity's service.

Is it laziness
to long for books
after dark ended labor,
to put aside the muscled
arms of hours pounding
the trudged miles of
bucket journeys?

Or do our dreams,
long sustained,
keep us human,
tender,
able to love?

~ *January 1995*

El Regadio is a vibrant agricultural community northeast of Managua.

MOTHERS OF MATAGALPA

Tears on bulleted bodies,
grief for the disappeared,
poor, abandoned, wellsprings of power,
tidal waves of reconciliation,
healing hands on festered wounds,
picked by politicians.

Monumental dreams, homes, jobs,
water, health, seed Matagalpa's soil,
piped by women's sweat,
hands, hearts, singing hopes,
street defended, prayer invoked.

Watch your head, Holofernes!*

~ *December 1995*

* *Holofernes* – Book of Judith, *Chapters 12 & 13*

COMPUPAN
(COMPUtadoras PAra Nicaragua)

Computers,
    mystery chips,
        the on and off blinks,
in a nanosecond's eye,
    that wink,
        uplink the globe,
world wide webs
    of electronic spiders,
        playthings, darlings,
star wars of the earth's mighty.

And in Nicaragua,
    a child's hands dance
        across recycled keyboards,
forging keys to open
    screened windows to the world,
        through which may pass a hope
that the poor, too,
    may inherit
        a share of the technological earth.

~ April 1996

El Niño Campaign

Rice,
stacked high,
100 pounds a sack,
bulging the truck
as it bounces
over stony roads,
to parched villages
where dusty eyes
light with hope
as they behold
El Niño's gift,

Today's Eucharist

~ *February 1998* ~

El Niño is a climate pattern in the tropical Pacific that causes floods and droughts.

NETWORKS OF HOPE

Hurricane Mitch struck in torrents,
    melted the land,
    leaving ruins.

A call, a caravan, a helicopter
    flickered the morass.
A human hive
    beginning to summon
Networks of Hope.

Hands, supplies, hearts reach out
    to heal, comfort, build, re-attach
    the ruptured sinews of the land
'Til hope proves contagious
    and the children cease to cry
    when it rains.

~ December 1998

THE COMMUNITY OF *FE Y ESPERANZA*

The gray ash plume of San Cristobal,
 the mudslide scar down La Casitas,
 the volcanic smoke of Telpanica
 backdrop new homes of *Fe y Esperanza**
 that embrace Posoltega's survivors,
 a refuge hugging refugees
 from Mitch's deadly rains and mud.

New street lights twinkle the night,
 cocoons of ball playing and circles of laughter
 switched on by the hands of friends across the seas
 who multiplied the blocks,
 stacked zinc roof panels, piped the clear water,
 and funded the land
 that Nicaraguan partners translated
 into loving space for those whose
 government loved them not.

        ~ *December 2000*

* *Faith and Hope*

A PhD Program's Promise

Dreams of learning mired by
    a thousand duck pecks of poverty.
Still the sparks hide smoldering
    amidst the dry tinder of hope.
Waiting, watching, dreaming yet
    of wondrous adventures that await,
    if only a tutor be found,
    a uniform afforded,
    pen, pencil and paper be wrestled
    from the UN's index of "extreme misery."

Then will dreams transform
    into a Program of Human Development.
Once-mute hearts will step lightly
    to the dance of learning
    and the heirs of Dario*
    will take up their inheritance.

        ~ July 2003

* *Ruben Dario is Nicaragua's most famous poet.*

CHALLENGE TO DEVELOPMENT

The nestling
picks at its pinfeather wings
then stands and strokes the air
with mighty beats,
its talons gripping tightly to the nest,
lest it fall.

Overhead the racing shadow
marks the falcon's passage,
delighting the thermals,
diving to opportunities
at the flick of imagination's sinewed wings.

The fledgling cries out,
"I believe I am called to soar.
Help thou my unbelief."

$\sim$ *November 2003*

YOU BE THE JUDGE

We were hungry,
> *And you helped us organize a school lunch program.*

We were illiterate with blurred vision,
> *And you sent us reading glasses.*

We were thirsty,
> *And you helped us build systems for potable water.*

We were poor,
> *And you helped us fight off CAFTA.*

We were homeless,
> *And you helped finance our houses.*

We were dropping out of school,
> *And you provided us with school supplies and tutorial classes.*

We were jobless,
> *And you capitalized our sewing cooperatives to make
> school uniforms.*

We were alone and disheartened,
> *And with your partners, the Institute of John XXIII,
> you accompanied us,*
>> *And took away our long loneliness.*

~ December 2004

ELECTIONS IN LATIN AMERICA – 2006

"Vote your conscience," say the idealists.
"Free and transparent elections," urges Jimmy Carter.
"Sharp penalties for Nicaragua if the people support the left,"
      warns U.S. Ambassador Trivelli.
"Harsh consequences if Nicaraguans vote against U.S. interests,"
      threatens Congressman Burton.

    Fears stir,
    a threatening grippe,
    as if the graves of young Nicaraguans
    and the bones of the martyrs
    were not sufficient warning of the *gringos'* intent.

    But we are living a new Advent,
    a Bolivarian* revival,
    the United States, distracted,
    seeking wisdom for the East,

    A babe is born,
    the peasants and workers hear the angel's song,
    to mark the ballots of their hearts.

                ~ *December 2006*

*Simon Bolivar was a Venezuelan hero who united South America
in a federation free from Spanish control in the early 1800s.*

DISASTER LAND

The gale swelled to category 5
    let loose the eye wall on the Caribbean shacks —
    an explosion of the aged zinc,
        green-yellow rays thru the forests,
        light saber from the ocean's deep,
    sawmill from the sky
    exploding limbs of pine, rosewood, mahogany,
        even the great guanacastes
    robbing the poor of their rice and beans.

Ay Nicaragua, Nicaraguita
    disasters' crossroads.
Teach us how you laugh again,
    and hope for the future,

How dare you dream anew that
    the seeds of corn and beans and vining squash
    will share the planting stick's fresh lair
    to feed the children of a new generation.

Let us plant the world together.

~ December 2007

Felix struck Nicaragua as a category 5 hurricane with 160 mph winds.

REYES SUR

"Will we ever see you again?"
        asked the Nicaraguan peasants.
"Many have promised much
        but never returned."

Three years of partnership
        have patched the doubts
        with deeds of solidarity.

Homes, latrines, public health care,
        leadership training, adult education,
        learning circles, school lunches, potable water,
have eased the hand of poverty
        and stepped lightly to the dream music.
Those who lived in misery have seen a great light.

And the shepherds said,
"Let us go over to Bethlehem and
        see the marvel God has made known to us."
A light of revelation to the Gentiles
        and the glory of your people Israel.

~ December 2006

Reyes Sur is a small impoverished community south of Managua.

MISCELLANEA

DREAMS

...are the good news of our imaginations.

They warm our hopes,
    recruit our passions,
        infect our lives,
    and make love our favorite color.

~ May 1995

9/11

The poet* said,

"I have always known
    that at last, I would take this road,
    but I did not know it would be today."

Our prayers and hearts are with you,
    our sisters and brothers of the New York area
    for whom these words struck special hope
    on morning wings of death
    that disappeared so many of your loved ones.

May our grieving land work through the rage
    and the trumpets clamoring vengeance.

May we wage a healing war
    on debt, poverty, hunger, disease and injustice
    that terrorize so many on our daily earth.

Until forgiveness and sharing
    heal hatreds and ensnare violence
    with a million strands of love.

                                        ~ *Fall 2001*

* *Narihira, 9th century Japanese poet*

LIGHT THE WICK

They said we are to love God
    and love our neighbors,
    a two-fold command to a lot of lovin'.

But Jesus asks more,
    a call to Action
    to love our neighbors, near and distant,
    as ourselves, the oft-forgotten,
    a bigger heap of heart-work.

Spiritual people warned us of the road,
    "You'll lose the silence,
    swamp the prayer time,
    noisy activists,
    clanging liberation gongs."

But the Good News is insistent.
    Hear the cry of the poor,
    "I will be with you all days,"
    Crabgrass Christians,
    Noisy Contemplatives,
    filled with the beatitudes' biases of Jesus.

Behold creation with the eyes of your hearts
    'til wax and wick are used up.
    whose life cries out,
    *Pega la mecha.**

                       ~ *From* Noisy Contemplation, *2008*

* *Colloquial Nicaraguan expression meaning "light the wick."*

HAIL, FULL OF GRACE

...Peace and strength to you —
Women religious of the United States,
and to the host of angelic spirits
who stand in solidarity with you
and await the song of Bethlehem
knowing that Jesus is nigh.

~ December 2009

Introduction to the 4-page ad supporting the U.S. nuns under investigation by the Vatican and published in the December 25, 2009, issue of the National Catholic Reporter.

CRABGRASS CHRISTIANS

We travel with a God who loves us.
We travel with a community of faith.

We'll often remember that
    we are crabgrass Christians
    whose love can survive
    in the cracks of life's sidewalks.

Our love reminds us that God's Spirit
    is with us all days.
We are blessed with a merry God.
    Indeed, we are the entertainment.

~ *From* Noisy Contemplation, *1982*

FAMILY & FRIENDS

TO DOLLY

You bring me sunshine,
warmth amidst the touch of autumn.

Geese cry earthward, questing winter warmth
while my heart lives joyous in
the tropics of your love.

~ September 19, 1971

DEAR DOLLY

I saw a pink sunset last week
   and thought of you
   as the sky grew fiery
   then slowly faded
   and turned to night.

I saw you Friday
   down bus stairs
   and into waiting arms and heart
   and hope that we might share
      life, faith,
      love, joy
   together and apart
      yet one
      two fountains of life and love
      playing life and calling growth
   from large children of timid heart
      and lack of faith
      in themselves
      or others
      or God.

I see you Sunday
   from engined carriage
      to a waiting heart
      that beats one with yours
      that twines its caring
   with your life,
      that joys in loving you,
      that finding you, now rests content
   to make life
   to make joy
      with you, dear Dolly.

~ Christmas 1971

JACKMAN

Bangor welcome – home to love,
    joy together
    sweet cell-dreams.
    Morning work-sharing, helping, caring.

Cyclamens, begonias, seeds of promise.
    Sharing fears, joy and love transform
        mountains, trees, lakes capped with
        ice bonnets.
    Moon and planet speaking enchantment,
    evening tension, morning comfort, acceptance.

Creating, sharing prayer and worship
    footsteps following in the snow,
    free air and feel of Dolly.

Noontime welcome, dialogic promise,
    goodbye,
    sharing joy, sharing love, welcoming us.
    Card, beads, plans – welcome birthday.
    Boston beckons, Washington after.
        Thoughts of love shrink miles.

~ January 1972

MERCURY WOMAN

Mercury Woman,
    quicksilver across the hardwood
        of my heart.

Dancing past my pickup fingers,
    slipping the arms
        of my outstretched heart.

To surprise me with a kiss,
    a hug – then gone again.

Leading me onward in contented, merry quest.

~ Christmas 1993

TEXTURED LIVES

Textured lives
    are built of daily moments
    turned and treasured facets
    of the ordinary
        that weave a sacred cloth
        for our hearts.

Jackman, Waldoboro,
    joined lives like technicolor
        leaves of dying newness.

And from that love came forth –
    infant wonders,
    adolescent wonderings,
    children grown too swiftly
        to adulthood's dragging dawn –
    steeped in wishes,
        and parental pondering
            at who shall emerge
            from the chrysalis of love.

Hesitant to claim credit
    for the artist's stroke
    or the stroker's lob,
    yet proud allies,
    offering a hand and craving
        blessings beyond the
        family's dowry to bequeath.

Still, life turns daily —
    the interpersonal kaleidoscope,
    the political wheels,
    School Board sessions,
    clambake communities.

The patient medicines of relief,
    paper news, the candy, cards
        and milk of life,

the dip of the pond's paddle,
arms stroking the waters
    of Bermuda's triangle.

The grace notes of decoration
    coaxing renewed merriment
        from the Tavern,
    flowers of life,
    whirred logs from the wood lot,
    calls to the broker,
    buried treasures in each other
        yielding secrets
        to the patient pickaxes of love.

And always, a welcome mat,
    the chronic hand of hospitality
        that wears the floorboards
        with visiting feet.

We who own those feet,
    pray for future years
    to claim renewed interest
    on the investments
    already banked
        in the mutual fund of your lives.

Eye hearts to celebrate anew
    the goodness and commitment,
    the Little Prince time
        you have wasted on each other
        that makes these score and five
        the prelude labor
        that has double dug the garden,
        and laid in rich compost
        for future harvests
        and organic growth together.

~ *October 5, 1994*

*For the 25th wedding anniversary of Betsy & Ted
(Dolly's sister and brother-in-law).*

DOLLY AT 60

Three score years.

Is life 2/3 full
    or just beginning to ripen
    into knowledge,
    into laughter,
    into freedom to be a smart ass?

Ally of whoever needs
    and whatever's needed
    to get life lived,
    with a trenchant quip,
    an intuiting heart.

And a wisdom befitting
    an elder crone
    or a holy woman.

But for God's sake, keep the homily short,
    and don't sing all the verses.

~ January 31, 2002

To Helen

A deft note,
    a fond smile
    a cup of tea at the kitchen table.

A heart that rises to the machinery man's calls
    reminds you
    that when you dig illegal clams,
    take a lady
    who knows the wardens.

~ *Christmas 2002*

Helen was an "almost" relative in Maine.

A BAD CASE OF THE GOOD NEWS?

Hearts reaching out,
> let not the left ventricle know the doings of the right,
> no phylacteries on the corner,
> nor trumpets at the temple.

But rather a family with a passion to help
> the broken heal, the hungry eat, the deaf hear,
> and the lame leap like the deer.

Can it be the Down East air, New Haven's ivied walls,
> or the Seattle mists that makes their hearts resonate
> with suffering people, the deprived, or the grieving?

Or might the rumors be true –
> that their house is badly infected by the Good News
> that has so warped their lives with Jesus' love for the poor
> that their plight is hopelessly hopeful?

Maybe the rumors are true.

~ *May 2007*

Written for Judy and John who are friends and benefactors.

To Jim

Jim Burchell and PeaceWorks –
  20+ years of collaboration,
  20+ years of building a river of boxes,
  a cardboard flow, the gift of many hearts
    beating through northern Jersey.

A symphony of sharing in Nicaragua –
  conducted by Jim whose vision
    and rough-it-in-the-back-of a pickup
    brought visit-range to Nicaraguan projects,
  and translated the need into details that Jerseyites
    might capture and gather for the next container.

To Jim and the Jersey PeaceWorkers –
  the music of your lives has touched our hearts.

~ July 30, 2009

Jim Burchell coordinated the Quest for Peace cargo container shipments.

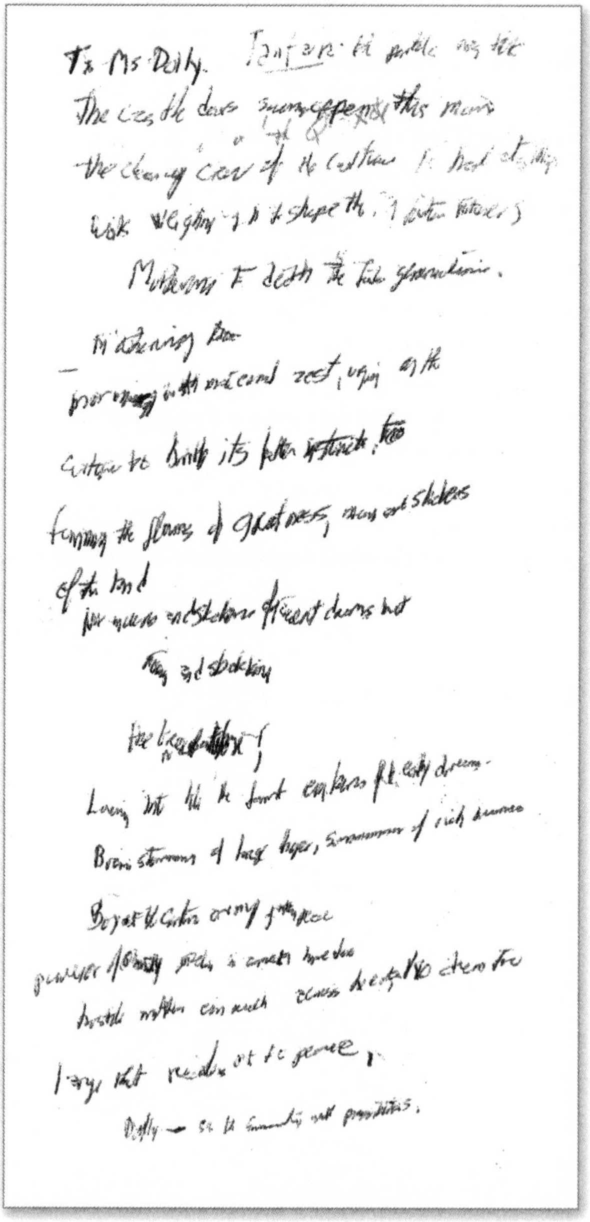

~ May 2010 ~

A poem for Dolly's retirement party.

HONORING BILL

PAEAN TO A GOLFER

By Bill D'Antonio, Bill's golfing partner

Oh, say, can you see?
Oh-oh — my ball hit the tree!
Woe is me! Woe is me!

Oh, say, look and see!
Bill C's at the tee!

His swing is a thing
    of beauty to watch
No tree does he hit.
It's all fairway for him!
While my shot leaves me grim!

Not Noisy Contemplation!
Nor Sancho's ruminations!
No — only quiet admiration
    as he drops a putt
    from thirty feet!

It sure is neat
    to play golf with Bill.
It's still a thrill
    that can't be beat,
    to admire his skill.

Thanks, Bill!

~ October 2008

Composed for Bill Callahan's retirement party.

DEAR BILL

By Tom Ricker, friend and colleague

It is quiet.
The world still
    in anticipation,
    taking a breath
    and considering
        what is to come.

Imagining a garden
    in Brentwood
    under deep blue sky,
    sorely in need of grooming,
        yet bountiful and smiling.

One can hear laughter
    on the grape vines
    and smell the sweat
    in the ground,
    released
        with the tug of a potato.

What comes next,
    when a life
    lived with joy,
    lived with passion,
    lived with determination,
    open hearted
    and purposeful,
        passes?

continued >

The world
    stops for a moment
    in anticipation.
And on the wind
    a booming laugh,
    a song off-key,
    a dream of justice
        leaves a trace on the skin.

Such a life
    is the reason for life,
    nourishing the ground
        so good things grow.

We say goodbye,
    thankful for your touch
    and the moments
        too few.

~ July 5, 2010

Written after hearing of Bill's death.

✦   ✦   ✦

July 2012 – Memorial service for Bill in Regadio, Nicaragua

A Brief Biography

NATIONAL CATHOLIC REPORTER

WILLIAM CALLAHAN, PEACE, JUSTICE CHAMPION, DIES

By Maureen Fiedler | July 5, 2012

William Callahan

Father William R. Callahan, an international leader in movements for social justice, peace, and reform of the Roman Catholic Church, died on July 5th, 2010, at Community Hospice Hospital in Washington, DC due to complications from Parkinson's disease. He was 78.

Callahan, a Jesuit until the early 1990s, was dedicated to the justice call of the reformist Second Vatican Council [1962-1965] in the Roman Catholic Church. He was best known for his leadership for peace and justice in Central America, especially in Nicaragua, and for his advocacy of gender equality in the Catholic Church, including women's ordination.

In the 1970s, he became a nationally known speaker on social justice and the spirituality of justice. In 1982, he published *Noisy Contemplation: Deep Prayer for Busy People*, which is a classic in contemporary spirituality. Deep prayer does not require the silence of a monastery, he said. Ordinary people can pray in the midst of noise and activism. "We are blessed with a merry God; indeed, we are the entertainment," he said in the book — with a flash of the humor for which he was famous.

His activism began after he entered the New England Province of the Society of Jesus (the Jesuits) in 1948. He pushed his community to take a strong stand for civil rights. In 1971, he helped found the Center of Concern in Washington, DC, a progressive Catholic think-tank dealing with global justice issues. In 1975, he launched Priests for Equality, calling for the equality of women and men in all walks of life, including ordination to the Roman Catholic priesthood. In 1976, together with Dolly Pomerleau and Jesuit Father Bill Michelman, he founded the Quixote Center, where — as he put it — "people could dream impossible dreams of justice and make them come true."

In the tradition of Cervantes' Quixote, Bill believed in "tilting at windmills" even when the world thought it foolish, reaching for stars that seem too distant to be touched. He often said that the work of justice should be done with laughter and merriment and creativity.

He turned his dreams into action, summoning thousands of people to join struggles for justice. He challenged his church on gender equality as a plenary speaker at the first Women's Ordination Conference in 1975. He launched the inclusive language project of the Quixote Center, which eventually published both the *Inclusive Language Lectionaries for Mass* and *The Inclusive Bible*, a non-racist, non-homophobic, non-sexist translation for common use.

In 1978, he began several years of ministry with Good Shepherd Catholics for Shared Responsibility, a lay group that had been disenfranchised by Bishop Thomas Welsh, in the then newly created Diocese of Arlington, VA. Welsh's policies had drifted away from the teachings and spirit of the Second Vatican Council, and these laypeople had been accustomed to active participation in their parish.

In 1980, Bill was silenced by the Jesuits on the issue of women's ordination, but resumed his public stance a year later. In the late 1980s, he founded Catholics Speak Out, a project of the Quixote Center that encouraged lay Catholics to take adult responsibility for the direction of their church.

In the late 1970s, he embraced the struggles of the poor in Central America, especially Nicaragua and El Salvador, becoming an outspoken opponent of the Reagan war policies in the 1980s. Together with Dolly Pomerleau, he directed the Quest for Peace, a multi-million dollar program of humanitarian aid and development funding for the people of Nicaragua who were victims of the "contra war" waged by the Reagan Administration.

continued >

Three times, the Quest for Peace set out to match Congressional appropriations of "contra aid" with humanitarian aid for the victims of that war. Callahan and Pomerleau mobilized grassroots activists across the country, and U.S. citizens matched a total of $227 million in war funding with the same value in humanitarian aid. For Callahan, "development funding" was not "charity;" it was a means to challenge injustice and change structures that keep people poor and oppressed.

He traveled to Nicaragua time and again, working with the Institute of John XXIII at the Jesuit University in Managua to channel the aid most effectively. He was an eloquent public spokesperson against the contra war, a stance which led him to testify in Congress against the economic embargo levied against Nicaragua.

In 1989, the New England Province of the Jesuits, at the direction of the Vatican, threatened Callahan with dismissal unless he severed his ties with the Quixote Center, Priests for Equality, and Catholics Speak Out, and returned to Boston. He refused to abandon his work with Nicaragua or for reform of the church. Consequently, he was dismissed from the Society of Jesus in the early 1990s, a move he strenuously resisted. It is not clear to this day what specific issue(s) motivated his final dismissal from the New England Jesuits.

In 1991, he became involved in the struggles of Haiti, calling for the re-instatement of the elected but ousted Jean Bertrand Aristide as president. He helped the Quixote Center launch a program called Haiti Reborn, providing aid for the poor of Haiti, especially in the area of reforestation.

Over the years, he guided many projects that the Center initiated, some of which spun off to become independent. These include: New Ways Ministry, a gay-positive ministry of advocacy and justice for lesbian and gay Catholics; the successful Karen Silkwood case on nuclear safety issues (completed by the Christic Institute); Interfaith Voices, a public radio weekly show; and Equal Justice / USA — a project opposing the death penalty.

In the last 20 years, although not a Jesuit, he remained a priest and ministered in several intentional Eucharistic communities in the Washington, DC area.

He was an organic gardener, known in his neighborhood for a plot that was somewhat jungle-like, yet highly productive. He lived a simple lifestyle. His bed was often a mat on the floor (next to the winter squash he had just harvested), his clothes were bargain basement specials or Nicaraguan shirts, and he was content to eat just about anything that wasn't moving.

He was also a dedicated runner. Even when his disease was slowing his ability to walk, he ran the Army 10-mile race (wearing a peace t-shirt, naturally). He called himself the "Parkinson Turtle" and finished the course.

Callahan received a Ph.D. in Physics from John Hopkins University in 1962, and was ordained a Jesuit priest in 1965. While studying for his doctorate, he worked for NASA and Goddard Space Center on weather satellites.

He was a resident of Brentwood, MD.

Callahan donated his body to Georgetown University Medical School, Washington, DC.

✦ ✦ ✦

PHOTO GALLERY

< Baby Bill

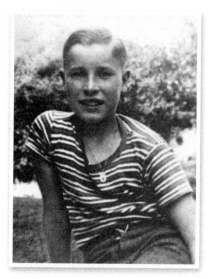

Young boy Bill

A dapper young man

High School graduation (1948)

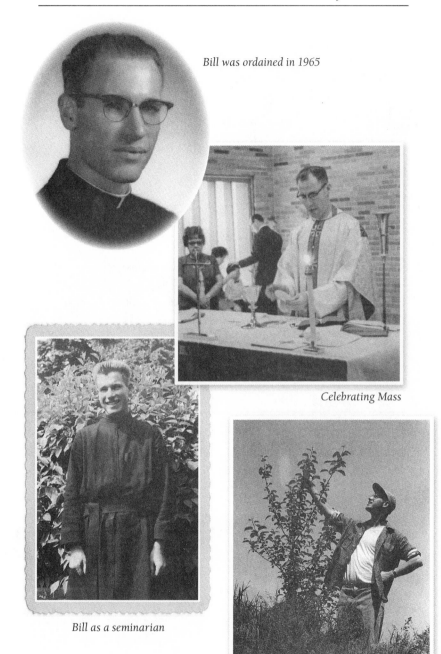

Bill was ordained in 1965

Celebrating Mass

Bill as a seminarian

In his apple orchard while in seminary

Bill in his 30s

In his lab working at NASA

Bill and Dolly in Boston

At the Better World Society award dinner for the Quest for Peace and other awardees. Ketxu Amezua, Chico Mendez (Brazil), Bill Callahan, and Bishop Thomas Gumbleton (1986)

With his parents and siblings

Bill with Dr. Jack Bresette
planning medical aid for
Nicaragua (1986)

Playing guitar with Mark Thoma Perry at
a peace rally in the early 1980s

Bill's tamed pigeon (1989)

Ketxu Amezua and Bill at a new
home dedication in Nicaragua

Demonstration for Peace

< Toasting the new edition of
Noisy Contemplation (2008)

At ease with family for Christmas

With Dolly at a Nicaraguan
Cultural Alliance sale

*Renovating the Quixote
Center's new home (1990)*

*Photographing paintings
in Nicaragua*

Celebrating the Quixote Center's
30ᵗʰ anniversary (2006)

Bill and Don Quixote in Spain

A messy desk, but a clear mind

Running the annual Army
10-miler wearing a shirt with a
peace message on the back (2005)

Ever the gardener (2008)

PUBLICATIONS FROM THE QUIXOTE CENTER

✦ *Inclusive Language Lectionaries*, 2008

✦ *The Inclusive Bible (the first egalitarian translation)*, 2007

✦ *Rivers of Hope*, 2007

✦ *Capital Defense Handbook for Defendants & their Families*, 2005

✦ *Let Haiti Live*, 2004

✦ *Rome Has Spoken*, 1998

✦ *Honduras: A Look at the Reality*, 1985

✦ *El Salvador: A Look at the Reality*, 1984

✦ *Nicaragua: A Look at the Reality*, 1983

✦ *Karen Silkwood: Union Sister*, 1978

PUBLICATIONS BY WILLIAM R. CALLAHAN

✦ *Noisy Contemplation: Deep Prayer for Busy People*, Quixote Center, 1982, 1994, 2008

✦ *Jason and Clytemnestra*, Quixote Center, 1983

✦ *The Wind is Rising*, Quixote Center, 1978

✦ *Soundings*, Center of Concern, 1974

✦ *Agenda for Justice (with Henriot & Ryan)*, Center of Concern, 1972

✦ *The Quest for Justice (with Henriot & Ryan)*, Center of Concern, 1972